Inside
Edinburgh

D1354853

GLASITE MEETING HOUSE

Inside

DISCOVERING THE CLASSIC INTERIORS OF EDINBURGH

Edinburgh

David Torrance

Photographs by Steven Richmond

BIRLINN

First published in 2010 by
Birlinn Limited
West Newington House
10 Newington Road
Edinburgh
EH9 1QS

www.birlinn.co.uk

Text copyright © David Torrance 2010
Photographs copyright © Steven Richmond 2010

The moral right of David Torrance to be identified
as the author of this work has been asserted by him
in accordance with the Copyright, Designs and
Patents Act 1988

All rights reserved. No part of this publication
may be reproduced, stored or transmitted in any
form without the express written permission
of the publisher.

ISBN: 978 1 84158 787 5

British Library Cataloguing-in-Publication Data
A catalogue record for this book is available from the
British Library

Designed and typeset by Mark Blackadder

Printed and bound by Bell & Bain Ltd., Glasgow

For my parents

STEVEN RICHMOND

*For my mother, who unconsciously
gave rise to this book by dragging me
around stately homes as a child*

DAVID TORRANCE

CONTENTS

GOVERNMENT AND CIVIC BUILDINGS

CHURCHES

MISCELLANEOUS

ST CECILIA'S HALL MUSEUM

INTRODUCTION

It has often struck me how little city-dwellers know of their own locales; familiarity may not breed contempt, but it certainly fosters complacency. Growing up in Edinburgh I was guilty of this myself, although two years living in London offered a cure. Every weekend and on occasional evenings I explored different parts of that sprawling metropolis, peering at exteriors and intruding into interiors wherever possible.

Yet the more I explored the more I realised that this was an indulgence alien to most Londoners. Many were fiercely proud of their city, and rightly so, but restricted their urban investigations to the areas in which they lived and worked, and even then to a limited extent. They regularly extolled the virtues of one of Europe's great cities, but actually knew very little of its character.

The same, sadly, is true of Edinburghers, who arguably inhabit the United Kingdom's second great capital city. Although not as architecturally rich as London – few cities are – the Athens of the North boasts a remarkable array of buildings, many of which go unnoticed by people who were born, raised and live in the city. The comparison with London is appropriate, for the inspiration for this book came from *Inside London: Discovering the Classic Interiors of London*, a sumptuous book originally published by Phaidon in 1988.

I was surprised, like the author of that book, Joe Friedman, to discover that a similar volume did not already deal with my native city. I came across books on Edinburgh's curiosities, its lost (and unbuilt) buildings, and even its graveyards, but nothing looking 'inside' Scotland's Capital city, behind its better-known façade. Bearing this in mind, I decided to write one myself. The next task was to find a photographer. I had known Steven Richmond since better-forgotten days of political activism at our respective Scottish universities in the late 1990s, although by 2008 (when we began work on this book) he was domiciled in London.

Gamely, Steve accepted what was nothing more than a casual commission with aplomb, making several forays north – at his own expense – to capture these interiors with a much-loved Hasselblad camera. As a Northern Irishman living and working in London, he set eyes upon all but a few of these spaces for the first time, yet photographed them with instinctive attention to detail. I think it is safe to say that we both found it an enormously rewarding, if occasionally exhausting, experience.

A picture, of course, even a photograph, can never really give a sense of a whole space or interior. It can only offer a glimpse, or a hint, of the room in question. Yet capturing historic interiors on film is a relatively recent activity. Only in the 1980s did a twin boom in photography and interest in interior spaces make it a widespread phenomenon. 'Even when the snapshot became a reality through technical advances,' observed Ian Gow in his 1992 book, *The Scottish Interior*, 'remarkably few people bothered to direct their cameras to the interiors of their own homes.' Furthermore, added Gow, 'Modern photographs of historic rooms can never possess the same immediacy because they betray later changes.'

That may be true, but then the aim of this book was not so quixotic. Rather it was to record, explore and, above all, inform. I thought I knew Edinburgh and its interiors reasonably well until working on this project, but the process simply served to highlight my ignorance. For years I had passed the Central Hall near Tollcross and wondered what lay beyond its rather bland façade. Through this book I got my answer: full of understated character, it was a meeting place for Edinburgh's Methodists, the sort of hall Margaret Thatcher might have visited with her father as a child.

A similar story was true of the Free Church College on the Mound. The Church of Scotland General Assembly building was familiar from my activities as a political journalist, but I had always ignored this unremarkable tenement next door. A journalistic colleague and friend, John MacLeod (whose father Donald was principal of the college), suggested it and organised a tour. Returning some weeks later with Steve and his equipment, we captured fine images of the Presbytery Hall, a surprisingly opulent interior given its context. At the other end of the hall (but not in this book) hangs a famous painting by the pioneering photographer David Octavius Hill of the first Free Church meeting following the 1843 Disruption. A nice connection, if you will, between a mid-nineteenth-century depiction of an interior space and the volume you now hold.

Most of the interiors featured in this book are, like the Free Church College and General Assembly buildings, Victorian constructions which lie smack in the middle of the city. This was not deliberate, merely an inescapable fact of architectural life, although some readers will no doubt consider the inclusion of Pinkie House in Musselburgh a geographical cheat. The general aim was to select lesser-known spaces, or at least those unfamiliar to residents of Edinburgh. I knew of some already, had always wanted to see others (writing books opens doors, if you'll pardon the pun), while a handful were flagged up by friends, relatives and colleagues.

Pinkie House and The Witchery represent the oldest interiors included within these pages, while others like the National Library of Scotland were not completed until the mid 1950s. Whatever their age, most of those responsible for granting access were charming, helpful and willing to allow caveat-free photography. Others, who shall remain nameless, were infuriatingly obstructive and curiously unwilling to allow the outside world to peer inside their secret (and often publicly owned) domains.

Steve and I also tried to photograph interiors which are likely to remain well preserved beyond the (hopefully) long shelf life of this book, although at least one – the A-listed Old Royal High School – is at the time of press about to be redeveloped into an 'arts hotel'. Although this will bring one of the city's landmark buildings back into public use for the first time in more than 40 years, the Glasgow-based Gareth Hoskins Architects will probably alter its old assembly hall, featured herein.

This also raises a valuable point about interiors – and their related exteriors – in general. Ed Hollis of Edinburgh College of Art (who was helpful and enthusiastic) has described a building as 'a capricious thing: it is inhabited and changed, and its existence is a tale of constant and curious transformation'. There are sections in this book on banks and restaurants, but many of the former are now the latter, most notably the splendid Grill Room at The Dome on George Street. The widespread use of ATMs has rendered cathedral-like interiors super-fluous; diners and drinkers now enjoy surroundings intended for bankers, borrowers and savers.

Many of the interiors in this book are by well-known architects, Robert Adam and William Playfair among them, while others belong to little-known or even unidentified designers. I have endeavoured to blur the boundaries, for both are equally instructive. 'Architecture, towns and building are some of man's most expensive activities,' observed the architectural historian Professor Charles McKean, 'and have always been powerfully symbolic.' Towns, buildings and archi-tecture, he added, 'reveal much about the priorities, culture, politics and living conditions of the past'.

Indeed they do. Included herein is Parliament House, a bustling hall full of clients and advocates that can trace its role in Scottish public life back to the sixteenth-century foundation of the College of Justice. Similarly, the candlelit halls of the Speculative Society connects today's debates with those of Enlightenment Edinburgh, when the society first met. The chapter on church interiors, meanwhile, captures both the mass worship of decades gone by and the very 21st-century problem of declining congregations and shifting spiritual priorities.

There is also, it has to be said, an element of nosiness – perhaps voyeurism is a more civilised word – in a book such as this. 'A longing to get inside other people's houses is so widely shared a human phenomenon that it cannot be explained in terms of aesthetic awareness,' wrote John Gifford in his introduction to Sheila Mackay's *Behind the Façade.* 'There remains the question, perhaps only to be answered by a foreigner, of whether an obdurate national character can be found in the great variety of Scottish interiors produced over the centuries.'

Can the same question be applied to the interiors of Edinburgh? I think it can, although one must be careful not to overstate the differences between characteristics, be they national or cultural. The photographs in this book illustrate the similarities between interiors in other cities and countries as much as they do the differences, just as the oft-referenced 'characteristics' of Scots and their English brethren are perhaps more similar than either would care to admit.

The British artist Richard Hamilton observed, 'Any interior is a set of anachronisms, a museum, with the lingering residues of decorative styles that an inhabited space collects. Banal or beautiful, exquisite or sordid, each says a lot about its owner and something about humanity in general.' Which is, after all, what makes exploring these museums – however large or intimate – so fascinating. Indeed, encouraging exploration was a subconscious aim of this project. To aid that there is a gazetteer at the end of this book, although sadly some of the listed interiors will remain off limits to all but the most determined reader.

In writing this book my aim was to satisfy personal curiosity while revealing a side of Edinburgh that isn't as well known as it ought to be. If I manage to get just one reader to pause as they pass one of the buildings photographed by Steve Richmond, or indeed others which were not but appear on sight to be interesting, then I shall have succeeded in my task.

VALVONA & CROLLA

Shops

ERNEST C. GOLL

Stepping inside this barber's in the Stockbridge area of Edinburgh is like stepping back to a time when settling in a chair for a short, back and sides was a much more elegant experience. Ernest C. Goll has barely been altered since it was established in the 1930s, although Raeburn Place itself dates from the early nineteenth century.

I.J. MELLIS CHEESEMONGER

Although the canopy of this cheesemonger's, also in Stockbridge, declares 'Est. 1993', it looks like it has been there for at least a century more. Iain Mellis, who opened this shop after working in the British cheese industry for 15 years, deliberately sought a traditional, old-fashioned style of service for an impressive range of, as the shop window says, 'Fine Farmhouse & Artisan Cheeses'.

GRAMOPHONE EMPORIUM

The Gramophone Emporium, again in Stockbridge, is a place out of time. Crammed full of old gramophones, shellac 78s and (almost grudgingly) vinyl LPs, it is a treasure trove of pre-digital music which I first discovered – by word of mouth – as a teenage collector of old discs. The shop on St Stephen Street dates back to the mid 1970s, when low-budget businesses took advantage of cheap rents. There isn't much space. A front room lined with shelf upon shelf of discs requires patience (it is only very loosely organised), while a disc-lined alley leads to a back room, which is again full of discs. Only open twice a week, it is a remarkably relaxing place to spend an afternoon browsing.

VALVONA & CROLLA

Scotland's oldest delicatessen, Valvona & Crolla, is an Edinburgh foodies' institution. Founded in 1934 when Alfonso Crolla joined the already well-established R. Valvona & Co. at its new premises on Elm Row, initially it served the city's immigrant Italian community. Produce is still packed into shelves right up to the ceiling, just as it was in the 1930s, to get around the lack of storage space. The shop also has a fascinating history. Shortly after Mussolini declared war in 1940, a crowd of anti-Italian youths smashed its original tall Georgian windows (one of which, partially obscured, can be seen above the entrance) and swept produce to the ground. Coffee dust rose like a fog while red wine flowed 'like a river of blood' down Leith Walk. Such scenes are unthinkable today, as well-heeled Edinburghers queue politely for their salami, cheese and pasta.

VALVONA & CROLLA

THOMAS J. WALLS

This optician on Forrest Road has, like Ernest C. Goll, the feeling of another age. The displays of designer frames (hidden in this photograph) should look out of place among the mahogany panelling and frosted glass, but somehow they don't. Once a bakery, Thomas J. Walls was fitted out in 1934 by the prestigious Edinburgh firm Heggie & Aitchison after Walls, originally makers of scientific instruments, bought the premises in 1933.

McNAUGHTAN'S BOOKSHOP

Established by Major and Mrs McNaughtan upon his retirement from the army, this charming second-hand and antiquarian bookshop on Haddington Place opened in 1957 and is probably the longest-running business of its kind in Scotland. Mrs McNaughtan continued to run it after her husband's death, but retired in 1979 and sold it to her assistant and its present owner, Elizabeth Strong. The shop is well stocked and has a particularly good Scottish books section. I never visit without buying something, including the occasion on which these photographs were taken.

THE WITCHERY

Restaurants and Hotels

THE DOME

Formerly the head office of the old Commercial Bank of Scotland, this Graeco-Roman building then housed a branch of the Royal Bank of Scotland before being converted into a restaurant and bar. Designed by David Rhind in the 1840s, the Grill Room (now the main restaurant) sits in the magnificent former telling hall, a Greek cross with arched ceilings and a central dome. The columns were originally marbled wood but in 1885 the Commercial Bank's new architect, Sydney Mitchell, re-faced them using Devonshire marble. The building also boasts marble mosaic floors with the Commercial Bank's coat of arms in the middle.

CAFÉ ROYAL

Already an Edinburgh institution, the Café Royal moved to this stylish Parisian building, designed by local architect Robert Paterson, in 1863. A glorious example of Second French Empire style, little has changed since then. Elegant stained glass and fine late-Victorian plasterwork dominate the Circle Bar and adjoining Oyster Bar, the most famous feature being six large glazed-tile pictures of famous inventors by Doulton, designed by John Eyre and executed by K. Sturgeon and W.G.W. Nunn. All came close to destruction when, in the mid 1960s, the building was nearly sold to Woolworths, which wished to extend its Princes Street store. Planning officers – together with 8,700 petitioners – intervened and in 1970 the whole building was listed, thus preserving it for future drinkers and diners.

CAFÉ ROYAL

SCOTSMAN HOTEL

The whole west side of North Bridge is dominated by Dunn & Findlay's Scotsman Buildings, although only the section facing Princes Street was actually occupied by the newspaper. I well remember visiting the mahogany-panelled public office of this intimidating building as a boy when my mother placed small ads in the *Edinburgh Evening News*. That is now a brasserie, but the most elegant part of the building (these days a luxury hotel) is the magnificent marble staircase, unseen by my childhood eyes, and flanked by an austere stained-glass window. One can imagine this and the entire building resonating as the *Scotsman*'s giant presses began to roll in the lower ground floor.

PRESTONFIELD HOUSE HOTEL

Originally a private mansion, Prestonfield House had already been converted into a hotel by the time James Thomson (who also owns the Witchery) took over. Built in the late seventeenth century for Sir James Dick, a former lord provost of Edinburgh, a modest vestibule sets the scene for the rest of the house, including the original drawing room, or Tapestry Room, which runs across much of the west front. There is decoration everywhere, but it is the deep plaster ceiling which sticks in the mind, featuring animals and pots of lilies surrounding a foliage centrepiece. Hotel guests can sit here, drinking tea and undoubtedly becoming slightly overwhelmed at all there is to take in.

PRESTONFIELD HOUSE HOTEL

THE WITCHERY

Originally Boswell's Court, this was built for Edinburgh merchant Thomas Lowthian in 1595. At the end of the nineteenth century the two lower floors were converted by Hardy & Wight into committee rooms for the General Assembly of the Church of Scotland, and indeed it is easy to imagine Victorian clerics arguing over obscure theological points by candlelight under the gilded ceilings. Now the atmospheric Witchery restaurant, the walls are covered in oak panelling – much of it rescued from St Giles Cathedral and a Burgundian château – and hung with tapestries, mirrors and carvings, while gilded antique leather screens, polished church candlesticks and red leather seating complete the opulence. Several luxury bedroom suites are situated across the road.

NEW CLUB

Clubs and Societies

ROYAL SOCIETY OF EDINBURGH

This building on George Street was originally designed in 1843 for the Edinburgh Life Assurance Company by William Burn & David Bryce and adapted for the society's use by W.T. Oldrieve in 1909. A gathering place for Edinburgh's intellectual elite, the Scott Room (Sir Walter was president from 1820 to 1832) is the Society's Council Chamber. The chairs were made in 1826 by the Edinburgh cabinet-maker William Trotter to a design by William Playfair, and designations for the officers can be seen on the back panels. The clock on the mantelpiece once belonged to the Edinburgh Life Assurance Company.

SNP CLUB

This corner tenement on North St Andrew Street was built in 1824 by David Paton and is now home to Edinburgh's Scottish National Party Club, the main space being this unusual Round Room. Pilastraded windows form almost half its circumference and give views north to Fife and west to the Scottish National Portrait Gallery. Although the interior has seen better days, it hosts regular talks by Nationalist politicians and less serious gatherings in the adjoining bar.

NEW CLUB

This is the interior which inspired this book, and is all the more intriguing because the dining-room panelling belongs not to Alan Reiach's 1966 New Club building, but to William Burn's 1834 original which was demolished to make way for these more modern premises. Sir Robert Lorimer's panelling (which acts as a showcase for a Raeburn painting or two) is therefore a fitting link between the old and new. Today members can still enjoy a cheap and unpretentious lunch in this gentlemanly setting.

SCOTTISH ARTS CLUB

Conceived as 'a place of reunion' for painters as well as a convivial meeting place for anyone interested in the arts, the Scottish Arts Club bought 24 Rutland Square (designed by John Tait) in 1894 for £2,100, of which £500 was raised by members. A booklet published for the opening ceremony in 1894 records 'the dignity and moral responsibility of Art in all its forms' and expresses the hope that the club 'may stimulate many to strong effect, and inspire some to great achievements'. That is certainly still the case today, no doubt aided by this fine dining room, which is adorned with paintings by previous members.

SCOTCH MALT WHISKY SOCIETY

28 Queen Street is a beautifully restored Georgian townhouse, handy for those visiting, living or working in Edinburgh city centre. Its suites of elegant rooms range over three floors connected by a sweeping staircase which ascends to a cupola framed by exquisite plasterwork. Whisky is featured to good effect in this photograph, showing bottled samples framed by a Georgian window.

SPECULATIVE SOCIETY

The Speculative Society, founded in 1764 during the Scottish Enlightenment, is dedicated to public speaking and literary composition. Forming part of the Robert Adam-designed Old College at the University of Edinburgh, the 'Spec Halls' were fitted out by William Playfair in 1817–18. Largely unchanged since, the meeting room features benches, tables, chairs and a lectern specially designed for the society by the cabinet-maker William Trotter, also known for his work at the Royal Society of Edinburgh. The eighteenth-century candelabra is believed to have been retained from an earlier building owned by the society on the same site. This room is lit only by candlelight, adding considerably to its already rich atmosphere, while the library relies on more modern means of illumination.

OLD CONSERVATIVE CLUB

The interior of this building, designed by Sir Robert Rowand Anderson for the old Conservative Club in the 1880s, was redeveloped a century later for use as a Debenhams store. Thankfully, its new occupant chose to preserve Anderson's splendid staircase (although it was shifted from the club's front door to the rear of the shop) which sits in a two-storey open arcade. Three stained-glass windows by James Ballantine & Son commemorate Disraeli (with figures representing Politics, Imperial Liberty and Literature). What Victorian Tories would have made of the premises' changed use is anyone's guess.

DRUMSHEUGH BATHS CLUB

This is the oldest private swimming club in Edinburgh. Designed by John J. Burnet in 1882, the main bath (which is 70 feet in length) has an open timber roof, seven Moorish arches on cast-iron columns and a mezzanine gallery for access to the diving board. The majority of shares in the company are held by subscribing members. In the past the waiting list was said to be two years long, but the club has been affected by the modern leisure industry, and its website now declares that 'New members are welcome and there is no waiting list'. Its rates, however, still ensure a reasonably well-heeled clientele.

FREEMASONS' HALL

This is the most important work by A. Hunter Crawford, who later joined his family baking firm as its house architect. The present Freemasons' Hall was built during 1911–12 and replaced an earlier building that had been on the site since 1858. The forbidding vestibule boasts black marble columns, while the Grand Committee Room (known as the Board Room) upstairs is adorned with paintings of past Grand Masters and decorated with home-made wallpaper. There is a carving of St Andrew – who also adorns the building's façade – on the fireplace.

FREEMASONS' HALL

TILES CAFÉ BAR

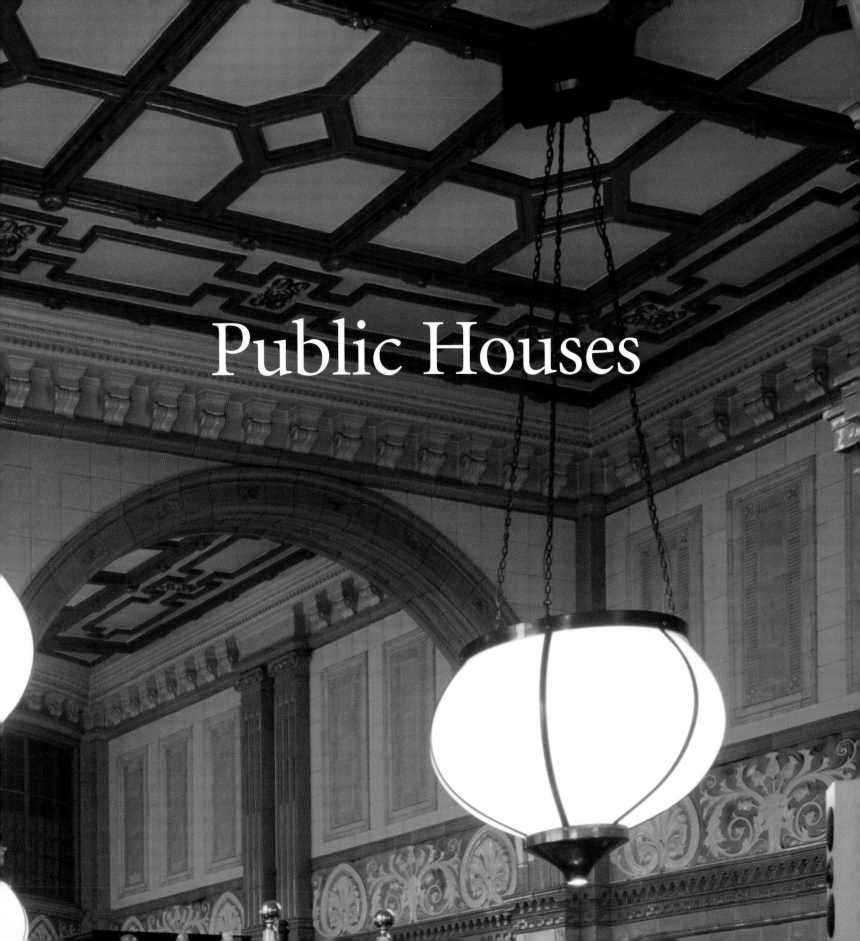

Public Houses

THE OXFORD BAR

Long a favoured watering hole for Scottish writers, the bijou Oxford Bar is now best known as the local of Ian Rankin's fictional detective, Rebus. Its literary associations date back to the first half of the twentieth century, when Scottish Renaissance writers would visit the bar and its legendary owner, Willie Ross. One of the best known of this group, Sydney Goodsir Smith, immortalised the pub in his 'Carotid Cornucopius', which Hugh MacDiarmid described as 'doing for Edinburgh no less successfully what Joyce did for Dublin in Ulysses'. Among the pubs featured in Smith's tour of Edinburgh's drinking dens, the Oxford Bar was easily recognisable to those in the know as 'Wullie Roose's Coxfork in Bung Strait'.

BENNETS BAR

This is one of Edinburgh's best pub interiors. The attrac-
tively long bar features an original tiered and alcoved gantry
which houses its whisky collection, and the brass water taps
remain in working order. Opposite the bar is a series of
mirrors surrounded by decorated tiles and carved wooden
pillars behind fitted seats. It has a wonderfully timeless
atmosphere.

KENILWORTH BAR

The name of this bar comes from the eponymous novel by Sir Walter Scott, whose picture adorns the pub's exterior sign. Originally a private house in Edinburgh's New Town, it was converted into a pub in 1904. The main interior space is dominated by an oblong central bar, brightly lit from windows looking onto Rose Street, but it is the tiled walls and ornate green ceiling that set this bar apart from others in the city.

LESLIES BAR

Dating from 1896, the red and pink tones of Leslies Bar immediately evoke a past era of genteel drinking. To the right of the entrance is a traditional bar counter while through in the snug is a wood-and-glass-panelled bar with four serving hatches rather like train station ticket booths. There's also a decorative ceiling with chandeliers to provide low lighting. Pictured is one of the separate panelled rooms leading off each of the bars which tempt punters with comfortable seating and small tables inlaid with brass and copper.

TILES CAFÉ BAR

Located on the south side of St Andrew Square, this building once provided office space for Prudential Insurance. Only marginally less impressive than its tiled competitor, the Kenilworth, Tiles Café Bar is an elegant setting for a post-work libation.

ABBOTSFORD BAR

Housed in a red sandstone block designed by Peter L. Henderson as a workshop for Charles Jenner (whose department store is just across the road) more than a century ago, the Abbotsford is another bar with a Sir Walter Scott association, although it is named after his baronial mansion rather than one of his novels. Its Jacobean ceiling and Spanish mahogany central bar has attracted the great and the good of Scottish public life, including actors, poets, journalists and politicians of a certain vintage. When the Royal Bank of Scotland's headquarters was still based on St Andrew Square, a young economist by the name of Alex Salmond used to accompany his boss here for a jar or two.

LIBRARY BAR, TEVIOT

This unusual bar is part of the first custom-built student union in the world. Spread over two levels with a balcony looking down on the bar, a tiny wooden spiral staircase and bookshelves add a scholarly air.

BUTE HOUSE

Domestic Interiors

BUTE HOUSE

This room's elaborate plasterwork ceiling is the great glory of Bute House, a restrained version of Robert Adam's own ceiling designs. Felix Harbord, the interior decorator who helped Lady Bute with her family homes, discovered the chandelier abandoned in the streets of Cleves, Germany, during the Second World War, and had it packed in empty munitions boxes and delivered to 6 Charlotte Square. Bute House is now home to Scotland's First Minister, who uses this room for meetings and receptions.

17 HERIOT ROW

Believe it or not, No. 17 Heriot Row represents a 'simpler kind of house' on this handsome New Town street. The engineer Thomas Stevenson and his son Robert Louis Stevenson lived here from 1857 to 1880, the latter being commemorated in a statuette that sits by the fireplace. Although it is still a family home, the house is hired out for meetings and conferences, and this drawing room is used for pre-dinner drinks and post-prandial coffee and liqueurs.

THE GEORGIAN HOUSE

Next door to Bute House is No. 7 Charlotte Square, designed by Robert Adam and built by Edmund Butterworth in 1796. Its first owner was John Lamont, 18th Chief of the Clan Lamont, who lived there until 1815. In 1975 it opened as the Georgian House after most of its rooms were decorated and furnished in simulation of their late eighteenth century look by the National Trust for Scotland. A fixture for school visits when I was a child, it was only on subsequent trips that I began to appreciate its meticulously restored interiors.

JOHN KNOX HOUSE

Whether or not John Knox actually lived in this house is a
moot point; the legend at least ensured the building's preser-
vation. This back room features a stained-glass portrait of
Knox by James Ballantine made in 1853. Dating back to 1470,
and now incorporated into the Scottish Storytelling Centre,
this Netherbow house was the home of James Mosman,
goldsmith to Mary, Queen of Scots, and tradition has it that
Knox lived here in the latter half of 1572. Due to ill health he
needed to stay close to St Giles Cathedral, where he
preached until his death in November 1572.

ADAM & COMPANY

Banks

ROYAL BANK OF SCOTLAND

This boardroom at the Royal Bank of Scotland's former headquarters is an elegant reminder that the financial superpower used to be a much more modest outfit. Originally designed in 1771 as a home for Sir Laurence Dundas by William Chambers, it was acquired by the Royal Bank in 1825. Of the original eighteenth-century first-floor interior only this room now survives (it was once the drawing room). Chambers himself possibly designed the woodwork and chimneypiece, while the Adam-style ceiling is by George Richardson. The portrait at the far end of the room depicts John Campbell, a diarist and cashier to the Royal Bank from 1745 until his death in 1777.

STANDARD LIFE INVESTMENTS

The Standard Life Assurance Company moved from the Old Town to these offices on George Street in 1839, although the original building by David Bryce was replaced with a new building in the neo-Palladian style, designed by J.M. Dick Peddie and G. Washington Browne, between 1897 and 1901. Pictured is its dramatic stairwell. After nearly 160 years the company moved to a newly built head office on Lothian Road and, following a refurbishment, this became head office of a subsidiary company, Standard Life Investments Ltd.

ADAM & COMPANY

The name of this modestly housed bank, Adam & Company, is particularly appropriate given that Robert Adam designed it in 1791, although the institution takes its name from Adam Smith, the economist, rather than the architect. An exclusive private banking division of the Royal Bank of Scotland Group, the simple yet elegant banking hall feels more like a reception room than a place to transact financial business. Upstairs is a series of more sumptuous meeting rooms.

ADAM & COMPANY

TALBOT RICE GALLERY

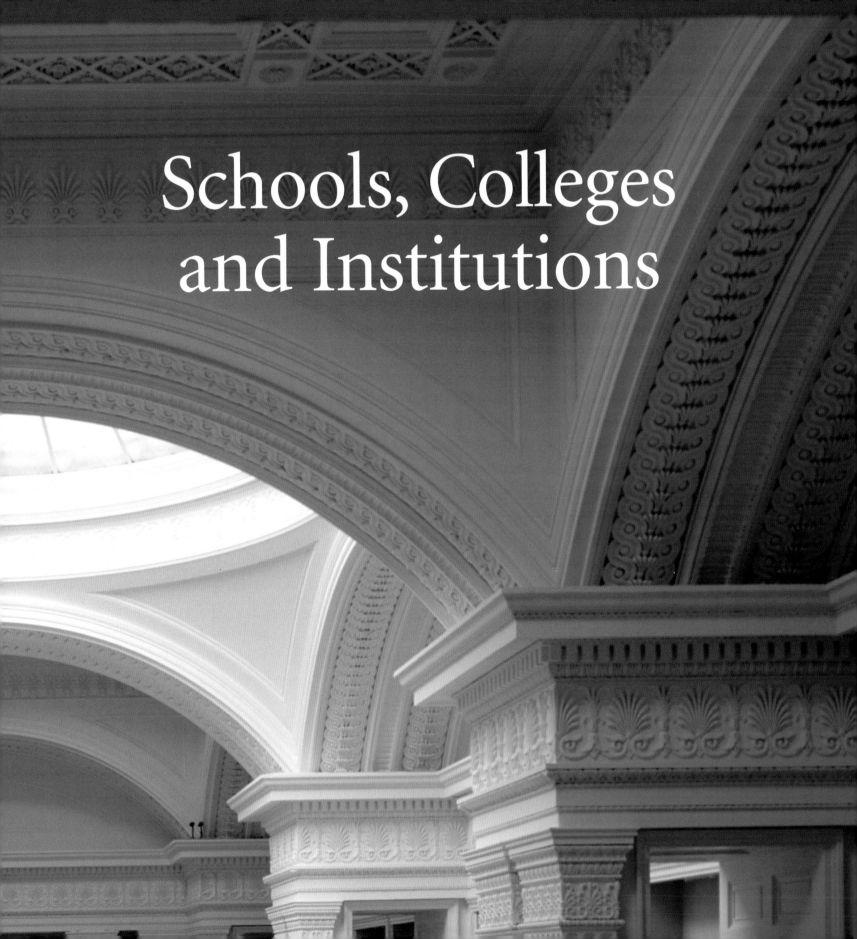

Schools, Colleges
and Institutions

SURGEONS' HALL MUSEUMS

Designed in austere fashion by William Playfair between 1829 and 1832, the Surgeons' Hall Pathology Museum is the oldest and largest in the UK, containing human anatomical and pathological specimens dating from the early eighteenth century. Developed as a teaching museum for students of medicine it has been open to the general public since 1832. In the same complex is the Royal College of Surgeons Edinburgh, of which the Fellows' Hall is the most impressive interior. In the middle is a coved ceiling with a glazed saucer-dome and leafy corner enrichment.

ROYAL COLLEGE OF PHYSICIANS

Thomas Hamilton's Royal College of Physicians is a hymn to neo-classicism dating from 1844. To the south-east of the building, and actually within No. 8 Queen Street, is the New Library, built to David Bryce's design in 1876–77 under the supervision of his nephew, John Bryce. The arresting ceiling, modelled by James Annan, has square coffers of engraved glass. Books are stored beneath the balcony in stall presses by Whytock & Reid. The corridor running from the New Library to the Stair Hall is particularly atmospheric, with its wood panelling and portraits of notable members. The whole building is one of only two Scottish buildings illustrated in Watkin's *A History of Western Architecture*, in which it is accurately described as 'eclectic'.

TALBOT RICE GALLERY

Established in 1975, this contemporary art gallery was named after David Talbot Rice, Professor of Fine Art at the University of Edinburgh from 1934 to 1972. This, the Georgian Gallery, was originally designed by William Playfair to house the university's scientific collections.

REID CONCERT HALL
MUSEUM OF INSTRUMENTS

This museum is in a side gallery of the main Reid Concert Hall, both of which were conceived by Professor John Donaldson, Reid Professor of Music at the University of Edinburgh from 1845 to 1865. Re-established as the Edinburgh University Collection of Historic Musical Instruments in 1980, on display are nearly 1,000 items including stringed, woodwind, brass and percussion instruments from the UK, Europe and all over the world. An intimate space, the crowded 1859 showcases create an almost Victorian atmosphere.

GEORGE HERIOT'S

The Council Chamber of George Heriot's was the last room
to be finished in the school's Old Building, in which the
original hospital was housed. The room is entirely
wainscotted with fine old oak, including a Corinthian
entablature. The fireplace boasts a finely carved mantelpiece
and a wreath of fruits, flowers and grain surrounding the
founder's arms. The room also contains an unusually large
gate-leg council table and two paintings, a copied portrait
near the window of the George Heriot, and nearer the door
a portrait of James Jackson, treasurer of the George Heriot's
Trust until 1804, painted by former Heriot's pupil Sir Henry
Raeburn.

FETTES COLLEGE

Fettes, perhaps Edinburgh's grandest public school, has produced two chancellors (Selwyn Lloyd and Iain Macleod) and one prime minister (Tony Blair), a fact of which it is justly proud. Perhaps all three dreamed of political glory in the school's Old Library, reached via an atmospheric flagstoned hallway. The David Bryce building was certainly intended to impress. Endowed with a substantial fortune from Edinburgh Lord Provost Sir William Fettes, Bryce's design was influenced by a trip to the Loire valley and Scotland's own baronial style, culminating in what a modern architectural expert has praised as 'undeniably one of Scotland's greatest buildings'.

FETTES COLLEGE

ADVOCATES' LIBRARY

The Advocates' Library is widely regarded as the finest working law library in the UK. Formally inaugurated in 1689, the status of the collection was confirmed in 1709 when Queen Anne's Copyright Act gave the keeper of the library the right to claim a copy of every book published in the British Isles. By the 1850s the library had effectively become Scotland's national library, William Playfair having begun work on its present home in 1829. The Faculty of Advocates donated its whole non-law collections (comprising 750,000 books, pamphlets, manuscripts, maps and sheet music) to the new National Library of Scotland in 1925, although members can still study the remaining legal texts under Playfair's fine gold-panelled ceiling.

SIGNET LIBRARY

The Signet Library was completed in 1822 in time for the celebrated visit to Edinburgh of King George IV, who described the Upper Library as 'the finest drawing room in Europe'. Photographed, however, is the simpler but no less elegant Lower Library, with its nave-and-aisles layout, Corinthian columns and small study tables. Both libraries are owned by the Society of Writers to Her Majesty's Signet (also known as the WS Society), one of the oldest professional bodies in the world. Its origins lie in the fifteenth century as the 'writers' of documents sealed with 'the Signet', the private seal of the Scottish kings, hence 'Writers to the Signet' or 'WS'. Nowadays they are more prosaically known as solicitors.

ANATOMY LECTURE THEATRE

It seems somehow inappropriate that the study of anatomy should have been provided with such magnificent accommodation. In 1874, when the building site for the University of Edinburgh's Medical School had been purchased and a public appeal launched, Sir Robert Rowand Anderson was selected as its architect. He had toured England and the Continent to study the latest designs, and his emphasis throughout was on the practical requirements of the interior of the building. His Anatomy Lecture Theatre, therefore, followed the traditional pattern with steeply raked benches rising above a central dissecting table.

PLAYFAIR LIBRARY

Along the southern side of the University of Edinburgh's Old College, William Playfair constructed one of his master-pieces, the Library Hall, now known as the Playfair Library. With its barrel-vaulted ceiling it extends to more than 190 feet in length, and is rightly regarded as one of Scotland's finest public rooms. It was used as a working library from the 1820s right through until the 1960s, when the university's main collection was moved to George Square. It is now used to host dinners, receptions and prestigious lectures.

PLAYFAIR LIBRARY

ST CECILIA'S HALL

Built in 1763 for the Edinburgh Musical Society to the design of Robert Mylne, St Cecilia's is the oldest purpose-built concert hall in Scotland. Here, the best and latest music was introduced to eighteenth-century Scottish audiences. This is the main Concert Room, its oval shape restored in the late 1960s with a shallow oval dome. Downstairs, the Museum of Instruments displays some beautiful early keyboard instruments.

McEWAN HALL

Before the construction of the Usher Hall in 1914 this was the city's main large hall, used not only by the University of Edinburgh for graduations but also for concerts and other functions. Designed by Sir Robert Rowand Anderson in 1874, the opulent interior decorations are by William Palin, who also worked on the Science Museum in South Kensington. The organ was a late addition and most of the pipes had to be incorporated into the existing platform apse. It is named after Sir William McEwan, founder of the well-known Edinburgh brewing firm, also a local MP, art connoisseur and noted philanthropist.

OLD ROYAL HIGH SCHOOL

Located on the southern edge of Calton Hill, the Royal High School of Edinburgh was designed by Thomas Hamilton and built between 1825 and 1829. Considered a key example of Scotland's Enlightenment architecture, this large oval space was the school's assembly hall. Its vaulted plaster ceiling has a very low curve, while rows of seats tier down to a central 'orchestra'. If it looks a little like a debating chamber that's because in the late 1970s it was refurbished to house a devolved Scottish Assembly, which failed to transpire following a referendum in 1979. Later it was used by MPs for meetings of the Scottish Grand Committee, while in 1999 it was again considered for the home of the new Scottish Parliament.

PINKIE HOUSE

Although a little outside Edinburgh, Pinkie House is a worthy addition to this book mainly because of the splendid Long Gallery with its painted ceiling. Added in the early seventeenth century to the existing building by Alexander Seton, Chancellor to King James VI, the decoration covers the entire 75-foot length of the ceiling and remains surprisingly well preserved. The Long Gallery has also enjoyed a colourful history. Following the Battle of Prestonpans in 1745 it was used as a casualty station (the bloodstains from the wounded are still visible), while Bonnie Prince Charlie spent two nights elsewhere in the building. Nowadays it is part of the less revolutionary Loretto School which, with a nod to Seton, counts two modern-day chancellors, Norman Lamont and Alistair Darling, among its former pupils.

DIVINITY LIBRARY

Founded in 1843 as the library of the Free Church College, New College Library now serves the university's School of Divinity. It is one of the largest theology libraries in the UK with over a quarter of a million items. When vacated by the Free High Church in 1934, the earth beneath the church floor was excavated to build three stackrooms. Many delicate wood carvings adorn the library fittings, and the stained-glass windows, designed by Dr Douglas Strachan, were completed between 1911 and 1934.

RAINY HALL, NEW COLLEGE

Although now part of the New College complex, the Rainy Hall was built in 1900 to mark the jubilee of the college's opening in 1850, taking its name from Robert Rainy, who was appointed principal in 1874 and who was also Moderator of the first General Assembly of the United Free Church in 1900. It was intended as a refectory for the college community and evokes an Oxbridge college dining hall. It remains the main meeting and eating place for New College students, most of whom probably don't notice the plaque commemorating Rainy and the coats of arms encircling them on all four walls.

GREAT HALL, EDINBURGH CASTLE

Government
and Civic Buildings

NATIONAL LIBRARY OF SCOTLAND

The National Library of Scotland was formally constituted by an Act of Parliament in 1925 but not actually completed until the mid 1950s. Designed in modern classical style by Reginald Fairlie (who called it 'frigid serenity') between 1934 and 1936, building work started in 1938 but by the outbreak of the Second World War only a steel frame had been built. This is the staircase that leads to the main reading room. The huge engraved-glass stair window is by Helen Monro to the design of A.R. Conlon (who finished the building), and includes inscriptions acknowledging the role of Sir Alexander Grant and the Faculty of Advocates in the library's creation. The figurine is of Thomas Carlyle. It remains one of only six legal deposit libraries in the British Isles and is a remarkably civilised place in which to read books and, in this case, write them.

NATIONAL ARCHIVES OF SCOTLAND

Designed by Robert Adam (while living in England), General Register House houses the National Archives of Scotland. Most of its interior spaces are very simply finished save for this, the main dome or rotunda, which is clearly Roman in influence. Seventy feet high and fifty feet wide, it is lined with calf-bound folios of the Register of Sasines. Both the dome and the plasterwork (by Thomas Clayton Jr), with its eight roundels, were refurbished in 2003–04 to house a new Family History Centre. Connected by a basement passage to the back of Adam's building is the Back Dome, designed by Robert Matheson as part of New Register House, built in 1858–63 to house registration details of births, deaths and marriages, the notification of which became compulsory from 1855.

NATIONAL ARCHIVES OF SCOTLAND

EDINBURGH CENTRAL LIBRARY

The great Scottish philanthropist Andrew Carnegie funded several libraries, but few are as impressive as George Washington Browne's Edinburgh Central Library on George IV Bridge, just across the road from the National Library of Scotland. Edinburgh was in fact one of the last Scottish cities to adopt the Public Libraries Act, already being well endowed with subscription libraries, and only in 1886 when Carnegie donated £50,000 did the city authorities acquiesce. A year later Carnegie personally laid the foundation stone of the new library, and he is commemorated here, in the main staircase, with an 1891 bust by Charles McBride.

ST ANDREW'S HOUSE

St Andrew's House has to be one of the most imposing buildings in Edinburgh, and also my personal favourite. Designed by Thomas S. Tait of the architects Burnet, Tait and Lorne, and built to consolidate and house a myriad of government offices scattered around Edinburgh, it opened in 1939 just as the world went to war. For the next sixty years it was home to the Scottish Office and Secretary of State for Scotland. One guide dismisses the interior spaces as 'dry and colourless Art Deco'. I beg to differ. Not only is the former Secretary of State's office (now occupied by the Scottish Government's permanent secretary) a walnut wood-panelled gem (legend dictates that it came from a single tree planted by Mary, Queen of Scots), but the magnificent conference rooms downstairs are also fine testaments to Tait's meticulous specifications. This one is pictured at full length, although pneumatically operated screens can quickly divide the space into three smaller meeting rooms.

THE MERCHANTS' HALL

Originally designed for the City of Glasgow Bank by David Bryce Jr (a nephew of his namesake) between 1865 and 1866, this beautiful space with its glass-coffered dome is now owned and occupied by the Edinburgh Merchant Company, which carefully restored the ornate panels and pillars. Plasterwork friezes depict the attributes of Trade, Industry and the Arts, while portraits and sculptures of the company's illustrious founders and benefactors also decorate the hall.

THE MERCHANTS' HALL

COURT NUMBER ONE,
COURT OF SESSION

Robert Reid designed the simply named Court Number
One, formerly the High Court of Justiciary, in 1835. A strong
Greek influence is present in the panelled gallery fronts, and
also in the compartmented ceiling with its large bosses. The
three round-arched Georgian windows lend the courtroom,
in which civil cases are heard, an appropriately judicious
atmosphere.

COUNCILLORS' ROOM, CITY CHAMBERS

With its eleven storeys stretching down to Cockburn Street, the City Chambers building is one of the skyscrapers of the Old Town. Formerly the Royal Exchange, the old Edinburgh Town Council took residence in 1811. Still the meeting place for plenary sessions of the City of Edinburgh Council, this is the Councillors' Room (formerly known as the Councillors' Smoke Room), which dates from the late nineteenth century and boasts armorial stained glass by Margaret Chilton and Marjorie Kemp, added in 1932. Busts of prominent Edinburgh politicians also add an intimidating air.

PARLIAMENT HALL

This handsome hall, with its hammerbeam roof of Danish oak, was the meeting place of the old Scottish Parliament from 1640 until the Union of 1707. Since then Parliament House, together with the adjoining buildings, has accommodated the Court of Session, and the stained-glass window to the south depicts the inauguration of this institution (then known as the 'College of Justice') by James V in 1532. When the court is sitting, this hall bursts into life, with instructing solicitors and clients mingling with promenading advocates. Parliament Hall is also adorned with portraits and statues of former legal luminaries.

GREAT HALL, EDINBURGH CASTLE

The Great Hall at Edinburgh Castle was completed in 1511 as the nation's chief place of ceremony and assembly. Commissioned by James IV, its greatest state occasion was a banquet honouring Charles I the night before his coronation as King of Scots in June 1633. For obvious reasons, when Oliver Cromwell took over the Castle seventeen years later he had the Great Hall converted into a royalty-free barracks. It was not restored until the 1880s, and most of the present decoration is therefore Victorian, although the hammerbeam roof is original and one of only two medieval roofs left in Scotland. The carved stone corbels supporting the beams are also the oldest Renaissance decorations in the British Isles.

GREAT HALL, EDINBURGH CASTLE

ST JOHN'S EPISCOPAL CHURCH

Churches

OLD ST PAUL'S EPISCOPAL CHURCH

Perhaps more than any other church in Scotland the history of Old St Paul's has mirrored that of the Scottish Episcopal Church itself, as the church literature claims, 'often embattled, at times romantic, on occasion triumphant'. 'Triumphant' best describes this distinctive building by Hay & Henderson, which sits on a narrow slope between Carrubers Close and the gloomy North Gray's Close. Its interior is dramatically atmospheric, the plain timber lining of the roof structure in stark contrast with its rich decorations, particularly a memorable Art Nouveau rood screen.

MANSFIELD TRAQUAIR CENTRE

Phoebe Anna Traquair spent eight years of her life creating the murals which earned this building the title of 'Edinburgh's Sistine Chapel'. The religious scenes, inspired by William Blake, were commissioned in 1892 when the building was a Catholic Apostolic church. The church provided scaffolding, met the cost of Traquair's tools and materials, and also paid her an undisclosed fee – the first time she had received payment for her work. The work was completed in 1901 and painstakingly restored a century later for what is now fittingly called the Mansfield Traquair Centre.

FREE ST COLUMBA'S CHURCH

The story of this church, the former Free St John's, is insep-
arable from the twentieth-century history of the St
Columba's Highland congregation – twice-weekly services
were held in Gaelic at St Columba's until the late 1980s. In
the building's post-Disruption period as Free St John's, it
was noted for the ministry of Thomas Guthrie (whose social
endeavours are commemorated in a Princes Street statue).
In 1907 – following tumultuous disputes over ownership of
Free Church property – it became the Assembly Hall of the
Free Church. Many original features of Thomas Hamilton's
1845 building remain, but the interior owes more to the John
Burnet & Son alteration of 1908, which transformed it into
the Assembly Hall. The austere interior is broken only by the
double-hammerbeam roof and Hamilton's ornate central
pulpit with its flurry of Flemish pinnacles.

FREE ST COLUMBA'S CHURCH

ST JOHN'S EPISCOPAL CHURCH

Built in 1818, this sumptuous church, at the west end of
Princes Street, was designed by William Burn, who chose the
then fashionable perpendicular Gothic style, most recog-
nizable in the plaster ceiling vault, derived from King Henry
VII's chapel in Westminster Abbey. Originally plain,
between 1857 and 1861 ten of the aisle windows were infilled
with stained glass, the work of Ballantine & Allan of
Edinburgh.

METHODIST CENTRAL HALL

When John Wesley, the founder of Methodism, visited Edinburgh in 1751 he declared it 'one of the dirtiest cities I have ever seen'. Nevertheless, in 1888 a young evangelist called George Jackson established the Edinburgh Methodist Mission and it grew so rapidly that by 1901 the Central Hall at Tollcross (designed by Dunn & Findlay) was opened. The interior is surprising, largely because it is so much more interesting than its rather dull façade. With seating for 2,000, it used to host 'cinematographic exhibitions' before Edinburgh had its first cinema. The city's Methodist congregation still gathers under the impressive curved ceiling every Sunday morning.

THISTLE CHAPEL,
ST GILES CATHEDRAL

The Thistle Chapel is the spiritual home of the Most Ancient and Most Noble Order of the Thistle, Scotland's highest order of chivalry. Legend dates it back to the ninth century, but the order was formally revived in 1687 by King James VII and contains 16 members, all appointed by the sovereign. Designed by Robert Lorimer and built in High Gothic style between 1909 and 1911, it is made entirely of Scottish material and contains stalls for the 16 knights, the sovereign and two royals. A wealth of religious and heraldic detail almost overwhelms the visitor. The windows show the arms of those who were knights during the building of the chapel and at the pinnacles of the seats are lavishly carved canopies with the helmets and crests of the knights rising above.

BARCLAY VIEWFORTH CHURCH

This unusual church, built for a Free Church of Scotland congregation, opened for worship in 1864 and was originally known as 'The Barclay Church' after Mary Barclay, whose legacy paid for its construction. The architect was Frederick Pilkington, described in *Private Eye* as Scotland's greatest designer of Gothic revival buildings, and indeed there is something almost irreverent about its heart-shaped auditorium. Pictured is the organ, designed by R. Hope-Jones in 1896, the pipes of which lead the eye to stencilled roof decoration by James Clark.

GLASITE MEETING HOUSE

The Glasite Meeting House was built in 1836 and in use until 1989, by which time the congregation had dwindled from around two hundred to six, and the resident housekeeper wanted to retire. The building was the first commission of architect Alexander Black, who built it to the Glasites' specifications, namely a simple design which reflected their belief that Christ's kingdom was purely spiritual and ought not to be controlled by the state. It's not difficult to imagine the congregation at prayer with uplifted arms, the box pews being so narrow as to make kneeling impossible. Services would last most of the day, breaking only for a meal, and psalms were sung unaccompanied, thus the absence of an organ. Even the low octagonal dome with its gold-tinted glass is austere. The building now houses the Architectural Heritage Society of Scotland, which has restored parts of the building.

SONG SCHOOL,
ST MARY'S EPISCOPAL CATHEDRAL

Specially built in 1885 as a rehearsal space for the choir of the nearby St Mary's Cathedral, the beautifully intimate Song School has been in almost continuous use ever since. Designed by John Oldrid Scott, son of the cathedral's architect, Sir George Gilbert Scott, the interior is dominated by a Henry Willis organ, but most notable for its wall paintings by Phoebe Anna Traquair. Commissioned by Dr Cazenove, sub-dean of the cathedral, Traquair agreed to illustrate the canticle *Benedicite Omnia Opera* ('O all ye works of the Lord, bless ye the Lord', from the Apocrypha), and covered each wall with processional scenes, flowers, birds, beasts and angels over a period of four years. An 1892 guide states that the 'idea of the decoration is to fill the place, so to speak, with visible song, to embody the rapture of praise, which is the highest expression of the spiritual rapture of praise which is the highest expression of the spiritual life of man'.

ASSEMBLY HALL,
CHURCH OF SCOTLAND

Following the Disruption in the Church of Scotland in 1843, the emergent Free Church of Scotland commissioned a complex of buildings designed by William Playfair, although this Assembly Hall was actually designed by David Bryce and built in 1858–59. Since the 1929 'Great Union' of the United Free Church with the established national Church of Scotland, however, it has been used by the Church of Scotland for its annual General Assemblies. This photograph shows the striking multi-tiered and galleried interior. Also visible is the Throne Gallery for the Lord High Commissioner, the monarch's representative. The Assembly Hall also has rich political associations. In 1989 the cross-party Scottish Constitutional Convention used the Assembly Hall to launch its 'Claim of Right' calling for the creation of a Scottish Parliament, which eventually met here from 1999 to 2004 while its controversial new home at Holyrood was being built.

PRESBYTERY HALL,
FREE CHURCH OF SCOTLAND
COLLEGE

The last thing one expects to find behind the unremarkable
façade of the Free Church College is such an opulent
interior. The ornate Presbytery Hall, designed by David
Cousin in the mid nineteenth century, has an impressively
coved ceiling with strapwork and pendants. The woodwork
is by J.R. Swann, while the west window contains fine
stained glass dating from 1862 by James Ballantine.

ST TRIDUANA'S CHAPEL

Originally the lower part of a chapel built by James III, this reputedly unique hexagonal rib-vaulted chamber housed the shrine of St Triduana, a Pictish saint who possessed the ability to cure the blind with healing waters which flowed nearby. The steeply pitched roof was actually added by Thomas Ross in 1906, and the buttresses (which replaced the original medieval structures) date from this refurbishment. Sadly, but perhaps also appropriately, the interior is regularly flooded by water, which is pumped out rather than used to restore sight.

ST BERNARD'S WELL

Miscellaneous

GLASSHOUSE,
ROYAL BOTANIC GARDENS

The Temperate Palm House, originally the New Palm House, was built by Robert Matheson (with a parliamentary grant of £6,000) as an extension to the original octagonal Old Palm Stove between 1856 and 1858. It measures fifty feet to the top of the stonework, with each glass dome adding another eleven feet. Slim iron arcades support the two superimposed convex roofs, under which several majestic palms thrive.

MANSION HOUSE,
EDINBURGH ZOO

Built as Corstorphine Hill House by William Keith, a wealthy accountant, in 1793, this building changed hands several times before coming into the possession of John Macmillan, of Melrose Tea, at the turn of the twentieth century. His initials (JM), and those of his bride (JFL), are engraved on the stained glass windows – which also feature figures of Art, Commerce and Literature – on the half landing of the main stairway; the window perhaps having been a wedding gift. In 1912, the Royal Zoological Society of Scotland purchased the house and grounds for £17,000, and today it houses the zoo's restaurant and meeting rooms.

DOVECOT STUDIOS
(FORMERLY INFIRMARY STREET BATHS)

Originally the Infirmary Street Baths (Edinburgh's first municipal baths) and designed by Robert Morham in 1885, this building now houses Dovecot Studios, Scotland's leading tapestry company, which has its offices and workshops in the old pool space where I used to swim as a child. The original pool gallery is now a viewing balcony overlooking the huge looms below. Having fallen into a state of disrepair, the space was sensitively restored by Malcolm Fraser Architects and re-opened in 2008.

ST BERNARD'S WELL

Tradition has it that three boys from Heriot's Hospital discovered the mineral springs at St Bernard's Well in 1760. In 1789 the owner, Francis Garden of Troup (Lord Gardenstone), commissioned Alexander Nasmyth to design a new pump house at the site. Based on the Temple of the Sybil at Tivoli, ten columns encircle a statue of Hygeia, while a mosaic floor and mosaic-domed ceiling complete the space. Last privately owned by the publisher William Nelson, his trustees offered the well to the City of Edinburgh as a gift.

CAMEO CINEMA

This independent film house originally opened in 1914 as the King's Cinema, becoming the Cameo following a 1949 refurbishment. Another revamp in the mid 1980s restored the main auditorium to its full Edwardian splendour, and it is now the only cinema of its kind still operating in Scotland. The Italian Renaissance interior could originally accommodate an audience of 673, and its lush abundance of ornate cornice work and plaster foliage is still arresting. I've always found the draped figurines, which spring from the columns and appear to support the equally ornate ceiling, particularly distracting.

GAZETTEER

The following information was correct when this book went to press and every effort has been made to ensure its accuracy. Readers are advised, however, to check opening times before making a visit to any of the buildings listed. Telephone numbers and email addresses have been included where possible.

SHOPS

ERNEST C. GOLL
Address: 28 Raeburn Place, Edinburgh EH4 1HN
Telephone: 0131 315 2137
Open: Monday–Friday 8.30 a.m.–4.30 p.m., Saturday 8 a.m.–4.30 p.m.

I.J. MELLIS CHEESEMONGER
Address: 6 Bakers Place, Edinburgh EH3 6SY
Telephone: 0131 225 6566
Email: stockbridge@mellischeese.co.uk
Website: www.mellischeese.co.uk
Open: Monday–Friday 9 a.m.–6.30 p.m., Saturday 9 a.m.–6 p.m., Sunday 10 a.m.–5 p.m.

GRAMOPHONE EMPORIUM
Address: 21 St Stephen Street, Edinburgh EH3 5AN
Telephone: 0131 225 1203
Email: info@rare78s.com
Website: www.rare78s.com
Open: Wednesday 2 p.m.–5 p.m., Saturday 11 a.m.–5 p.m.

VALVONA & CROLLA
Address: 19 Elm Row, Edinburgh EH7 4AA
Telephone: 0131 556 6066
Email: sales@valvonacrolla.co.uk
Website: www.valvonacrolla.co.uk
Open: Monday–Thursday 8.30 a.m.–6 p.m., Friday–Saturday 8 a.m.–6 p.m., Sunday 10.30 a.m.–4 p.m (June–December, Friday–Saturday 8 a.m.–6.30 p.m.)

THOMAS J. WALLS
Address: 35 Forrest Road, Edinburgh EH1 2QT
Telephone: 0131 225 7242
Open: Monday–Friday 9 a.m.–5 p.m., Saturday 9 a.m.–12 noon.

McNAUGHTAN'S BOOKSHOP
Address: 3a & 4a Haddington Place, Edinburgh EH7 4AE
Telephone: 0131 556 5897
Email: enquiries@mcnaughtansbookshop.com
Website: www.mcnaughtansbookshop.com
Open: Tuesday–Saturday 11 a.m.–5 p.m.

RESTAURANTS AND HOTELS

THE DOME
Address: 14 George Street, Edinburgh EH2 2PF
Telephone: 0131 624 8624
Email: sales@thedomeedinburgh.com
Website: www.thedomeedinburgh.com
Open: Daily from 12 noon–late.

CAFÉ ROYAL
Address: 19 West Register Street, Edinburgh EH2 2AA
Telephone: 0131 556 1884
Email: info@caferoyal.org.uk
Website: www.caferoyal.org.uk
Open: Sunday 12.30 a.m.–11 p.m., Monday–Wednesday 11 a.m.–11 p.m., Thursday–Saturday 11 a.m.–12 midnight.

SCOTSMAN HOTEL
Address: 20 North Bridge, Edinburgh, EH1 1TR
Telephone: 0131 556 5565
Email: reservations@thescotsmanhotel.co.uk
Website: www.thescotsmanhotel.co.uk
Open: 24 hours for guests or by appointment.

PRESTONFIELD HOUSE HOTEL
Address: Priestfield Road, Edinburgh EH16 5UT
Telephone: 0131 662 2323
Email: events@prestonfield.com
Website: www.prestonfield.com
Open: 24 hours for guests or by appointment.

THE WITCHERY
Address: Castlehill, The Royal Mile, Edinburgh EH1 2NF
Telephone: 0131 225 0976
Email: mr@prestonfield.com
Website: www.thewitchery.com
Open: Daily for lunch 12 noon–4 p.m. (last reservation) and dinner 5.30 p.m.–11.30 p.m. (last reservation).

CLUBS AND SOCIETIES

ROYAL SOCIETY OF EDINBURGH
Address: 22–26 George Street, Edinburgh EH2 2PQ
Telephone: 0131 240 5000
Email: rooms@royalsoced.org.uk
Website: www.royalsoced.org.uk
Admission: By appointment.

SNP CLUB
Address: 16 North St Andrew St, Edinburgh EH2 1HJ
Telephone: 0131 556 2656
Website: www.snp.org
Admission: Members only or by appointment.

NEW CLUB
Address: 86 Princes Street, Edinburgh EH2 2BB
Telephone: 0131 226 4881
Email: info@newclub.co.uk
Website: www.newclub.co.uk
Admission: Members only or by appointment.

SCOTTISH ARTS CLUB
Address: 24 Rutland Square, Edinburgh EH1 2BW
Telephone: 0131 229 8157
Email: scottishartsclub@btconnect.com
Website: www.scottishartsclub.co.uk
Admission: Tuesday–Saturday 11 a.m.–11 p.m. for members.

SCOTCH MALT WHISKY SOCIETY
Address: 28 Queen Street, Edinburgh EH2 1JX
Telephone: 0131 220 2044
Email: queenstreet@smws.com
Website: www.smws.co.uk
Admission: Monday–Wednesday 9 a.m.–11 p.m., Thursday–Saturday 9 a.m.–12 midnight, Sunday 11 a.m.–9 p.m. for members.

SPECULATIVE SOCIETY
Address: Old College, Edinburgh
Admission: Not open to the general public.

OLD CONSERVATIVE CLUB (DEBENHAMS)
Address: 109 Princes Street, Edinburgh EH2 3AA
Telephone: 0844 561 6161
Email: press.office@debenhams.com
Website: www.debenhams.com
Open: Monday–Wednesday 9.30 a.m.–6 p.m.,
     Thursday 9.30 a.m.–8 p.m., Friday 9.30 a.m.–6.30
     p.m., Saturday 9 a.m.–6.30 p.m.,
     Sunday 11 a.m.–6 p.m.

DRUMSHEUGH BATHS CLUB
Address: 5 Belford Road,
     Edinburgh EH4 3BL
Telephone: 0131 225 2200
Email: manager@drumsheughbaths.com
Website: www.drumsheughbaths.com
Admission: Members only or by appointment.
     Monday–Friday 6.30 a.m.–9 p.m.,
     Saturday–Sunday 8.30 a.m.–8 p.m.

FREEMASONS' HALL
Address: 96 George Street,
     Edinburgh EH2 3DH
Telephone: 0131 225 5577
Email: curator@grandlodgescotland.org
Website: www.grandlodgescotland.com
Admission: Weekday tours at 10 a.m. and 2 p.m.
     Telephone to book in advance.

PUBLIC HOUSES

THE OXFORD BAR
Address: 8 Young Street,
     Edinburgh EH2 4JB
Telephone: 0131 539 7119
Website: www.oxfordbar.com
Open: Monday–Thursday 11 a.m.–12 midnight,
     Friday–Saturday 11 a.m.–12.30 a.m.,
     Sunday 12:30 p.m.–11 p.m.

BENNETS BAR
Address: 8 Leven St, Edinburgh EH3 9LG
Telephone: 0131 229 5143
Email: bennetsbar@hotmail.co.uk
Open: Daily, 12 noon–1 a.m. (earlier on Sunday).

KENILWORTH BAR
Address: 152–154 Rose Street, Edinburgh EH2 3JD
Telephone: 0131 226 1773
Website: www.nicholsonspubs.co.uk/thekenil-
     worthrosestreetedinburgh
Open: Monday–Saturday 11 a.m.–11 p.m.,
     Sunday 12.30 p.m.–11 p.m.

LESLIES BAR
Address: 45 Ratcliffe Terrace, Edinburgh EH9 1SU
Telephone: 0131 667 7205
Email: lesliesbar@dmstewart.com
Website: www.lesliesbar.com
Open: Monday–Saturday 11 a.m.–12 midnight,
     Sunday 12 noon–11.30 p.m.

TILES CAFÉ BAR
Address: 1 St Andrew Square,
     Edinburgh EH2 2BD
Telephone: 0131 558 1507
Open: Monday–Friday 10:30 a.m.–12 midnight,
     Saturday 10 a.m.–12 midnight,
     Sunday 11 a.m.–11 p.m.

ABBOTSFORD BAR
Address: 3–5 Rose Street, Edinburgh EH2 2PR
Telephone: 0131 225 5276
Email: theabbotsford@dmstewart.com
Website: www.theabbotsford.com
Open: Monday–Saturday 11 a.m.–12 midnight,
     Sunday 12 noon–11.30 p.m.

LIBRARY BAR, TEVIOT
Address: 13 Bristo Square, Edinburgh EH8 9AJ
Telephone: 0131 650 4673
Website: www.eusa.ed.ac.uk/union/teviot
Open: Monday–Thursday 11 a.m.–1 a.m.,
     Friday–Saturday 11 a.m.–3 a.m.,
     Sunday 12 noon–12 midnight.

DOMESTIC INTERIORS

BUTE HOUSE
Address: 6 Charlotte Square,
     Edinburgh EH2 4DR
Telephone: 0131 556 8400
Email: scottish.ministers@scotland.gsi.gov.uk
Website: www.scotland.gov.uk/News/News-Extras/134
Admission: Closed to the general public.

17 HERIOT ROW
Address: 17 Heriot Row, Edinburgh EH3 6HP
Telephone: 0131 556 1896
Email: mail@stevenson-house.co.uk
Website: www.stevenson-house.co.uk
Admission: Only open for organised events or
     bed & breakfast.

THE GEORGIAN HOUSE
Address: 7 Charlotte Square, Edinburgh EH2 4DR
Telephone: 0844 493 2117
Email: thegeorgianhouse@nts.org.uk
Website: www.nts.org.uk/Property/56/
Admission: Daily; June 10 a.m.–5 p.m., July–August 10
     a.m.–6 p.m., September–October 10 a.m.–5 p.m.,
     November 11 a.m.–3 p.m.

JOHN KNOX HOUSE
Address: 43 High Street, Edinburgh EH1 1SR
Telephone: 0131 556 9579
Email: reception@scottishstorytellingcentre.com
Website: www.scottishstorytellingcentre.co.uk/john_
     knox_house/scottish_storytelling_jkhouse.asp
Admission: Monday–Saturday, 10 a.m.–6 p.m.
     (July–August also Sunday 12 noon-6 p.m.)

BANKS

ROYAL BANK OF SCOTLAND
Address: 36 St Andrew Square, Edinburgh EH2 2YB
Telephone: 0131 556 8555
Website: www.rbs.com/home.ashx
Open: Monday–Friday 9.15 a.m.–4.45 p.m.,
     (except Wednesday 9.45 a.m.–4.45 p.m.),
     Saturday 10 a.m.–3 p.m.

STANDARD LIFE INVESTMENTS
Address: 1 George Street, Edinburgh EH2 2LL
Telephone: 0845 606 0062
Email: investments_marketline@standardlife.com
Website: www.standardlifeinvestments.com
Open: Office hours or by appointment.

ADAM & COMPANY
Address: 22 Charlotte Square, Edinburgh EH2 4DF
Telephone: 0131 225 8484
Email: enquiriesedinburgh@Adambank.com
Website: www.adambank.com
Open: Office hours or by appointment.

SCHOOLS, COLLEGES AND INSTITUTIONS

SURGEONS' HALL MUSEUMS
Address: Nicolson Street, Edinburgh EH8 9DW
Telephone: 0131 527 1649
Email: museum@rcsed.ac.uk
Website: www.museum.rcsed.ac.uk
Admission: Weekdays 12 noon-4 p.m.

ROYAL COLLEGE OF PHYSICIANS
Address: 9 Queen Street, Edinburgh EH2 1JQ
Telephone: 0131 225 7324
Email: reception@rcpe.ac.uk
Website: www.rcpe.ac.uk
Admission: By appointment.

TALBOT RICE GALLERY
Address: Old College, South Bridge,
     Edinburgh EH8 9YL
Telephone: 0131 650 2210
Email: info.talbotrice@ed.ac.uk
Website: www.trg.ed.ac.uk
Admission: Tuesday–Saturday 10 a.m.–5 p.m.

REID CONCERT HALL
MUSEUM OF INSTRUMENTS
Address: Bristo Square, Edinburgh EH8 9AG
Telephone: 0131 651 2189
Email: euchmi@ed.ac.uk
Website: www.music.ed.ac.uk/euchmi/rch
Admission: Saturday 10 a.m.–1 p.m.,
Wednesday 3 p.m.–5 p.m., and weekdays
during August 2 p.m.–5 p.m.

GEORGE HERIOT'S
Address: Lauriston Place, Edinburgh EH3 9EQ
Telephone: 0131 229 7263
Email: enquiries@georgeheriots.com
Website: www.george-heriots.com
Admission: Not open to the general public.

FETTES COLLEGE
Address: Carrington Road, Edinburgh EH4 1QX
Telephone: 0131 332 2281
Email: enquiries@fettes.com
Website: www.fettes.com
Admission: Not open to the general public.

ADVOCATES' LIBRARY
Address: Parliament House, Edinburgh EH1 1RF
Telephone: 0131 226 5071
Email: enquiries@nls.uk
Website: www.advocates.org.uk/library/index.html
Admission: Not open to the general public.

SIGNET LIBRARY
Address: Parliament Square, Edinburgh EH1 1RF
Telephone: 0131 220 3249
Email: events@thesignetlibrary.co.uk
Website: www.thesignetlibrary.co.uk
Admission: Not open to the general public.

ANATOMY LECTURE THEATRE
Address: Doorway 3, Medical School,
Teviot Place, Edinburgh EH8 9AG
Telephone: 0131 650 2252
Email: communications.office@ed.ac.uk
Website: websiterepository.ed.ac.uk/explore/places/
buildings/anatomylecture.html
Admission: By guided tour only.

PLAYFAIR LIBRARY
Address: Old College, South Bridge,
Edinburgh EH8 9YL
Telephone: 0131 650 2252
Email: communications.office@ed.ac.uk
Website: websiterepository.ed.ac.uk/explore/places/
buildings/playfair.html
Admission: By guided tour only.

ST CECILIA'S HALL
Address: Niddry Street,
Edinburgh EH1 1LJ
Telephone: 0131 650 2252
Email: communications.office@ed.ac.uk
Websites: www.music.ed.ac.uk/euchmi/sch (Museum),
websiterepository.
ed.ac.uk/explore/places/buildings/
stceciliashall.html (Hall)
Admission: Hall and Museum, Wednesday and Saturday
2 p.m.–5 p.m. (During Edinburgh International
Festival Monday–Saturday 10:30 a.m.–12:30 p.m.)

McEWAN HALL
Address: Teviot Place, Edinburgh
Telephone: 0131 650 2252
Email: communications.office@ed.ac.uk
Website: websiterepository.ed.ac.uk/explore/places/
buildings/mcewanhall.html
Admission: By guided tour only.

OLD ROYAL HIGH SCHOOL
Address: Regent Terrace, Edinburgh
Telephone: 0131 200 2000
Email: frank.donoghue@edinburgh.gov.uk
Admission: By appointment.

PINKIE HOUSE
Address: Linkfield Road, Musselburgh,
East Lothian EH21 7RE
Telephone: 0131 653 4444
Email: headmaster@loretto.com
Website: www.lorettoschool.co.uk
Admission: By appointment.

DIVINITY LIBRARY
Address: New College, 1 Mound Place,
Edinburgh EH1 2LU
Telephone: 0131 650 8957
Email: new.college.library@ed.ac.uk
Website: www.ed.ac.uk/schools-departments/infor-
mation-services/services/library-museum-
gallery/using-library/lib-locate/newcoll-lib
Admission: For students, October–April, Monday–
Thursday 9 a.m.–6 p.m., Friday 9 a.m.–5 p.m.,
Saturday 12 noon–5 p.m.; May–September,
Monday–Friday 9 a.m.–5 p.m.

RAINY HALL, NEW COLLEGE
Address: 1 Mound Place, Edinburgh EH1 2LX
Telephone: 0131 650 8959
Email: divinity@ed.ac.uk
Website: websiterepository.ed.ac.uk/explore/
places/buildings/newcollege.html
Admission: By appointment.

GOVERNMENT AND CIVIC BUILDINGS

NATIONAL LIBRARY OF SCOTLAND
Address: George IV Bridge, Edinburgh EH1 1EW
Telephone: 0131 623 3700
Email: enquiries@nls.uk
Website: www.nls.uk
Admission: For readers, Monday–Friday
9.30 a.m.–8.30 p.m. (except Wednesday
10 a.m.–8.30 p.m.), Saturday 9.30 a.m.–1 p.m.

NATIONAL ARCHIVES OF SCOTLAND
Address: HM General Register House, 2 Princes Street,
Edinburgh EH1 3YY
Telephone: 0131 535 1314
Email: enquiries@nas.gov.uk
Website: www.nas.gov.uk
Admission: For readers, Monday–Friday
9 a.m.–4.45 p.m.

EDINBURGH CENTRAL LIBRARY
Address: 9 George IV Bridge, Edinburgh EH1 1EG
Telephone: 0131 242 8000
Email: eclis@edinburgh.gov.uk
Website: www.edinburgh.gov.uk/internet/Leisure/
Libraries/Your_nearest_library/Central%20Library
Admission: Monday–Thursday 10 a.m.–8 p.m.,
Friday 10 a.m.–5 p.m., Saturday 9 a.m.–1 p.m.

ST ANDREW'S HOUSE
Address: Regent Road, Edinburgh EH1 3DG
Telephone: 0131 556 8400
Email: ceu@scotland.gsi.gov.uk
Website: www.scotland.gov.uk/About/Contacts/
General-Enquiries/Locations/St-Andrews-House-1
Admission: Not open to the general public.

THE MERCHANTS' HALL
Address: 22 Hanover Street, Edinburgh EH2 2EP
Telephone: 0131 225 7202
Email: susan.walsh@mcoe.org.uk
Website: www.merchantshall.co.uk
Admission: By appointment.

COURT NUMBER ONE, COURT OF SESSION
Address: Court of Session, Parliament House,
Parliament Square, Edinburgh EH1 1RQ
Telephone: 0131 225 2595
Email: supreme.courts@scotcourts.gov.uk
Website: www.scotcourts.gov.uk/session/index.asp
Admission: Not open to the general public.

COUNCILLORS' ROOM
Address: City of Edinburgh Council, City Chambers,
High Street, Edinburgh EH1 1YJ
Telephone: 0131 200 2323
Email: justask@edinburgh.gov.uk
Website: www.edinburgh.gov.uk
Admission: Not open to the general public.

PARLIAMENT HALL
Address: Parliament Square, Edinburgh EH1 1RQ
Telephone: 0131 225 2595
Admission: Monday–Friday 10 a.m.–4.30 p.m.

GREAT HALL, EDINBURGH CASTLE
Address: Castlehill, Edinburgh EH1 2NG
Telephone: 0131 225 9846
Email: hs.ticketing@scotland.gsi.gov.uk
Website: www.edinburghcastle.gov.uk
Admission: Daily; April–September 9.30 a.m.–6 p.m.,
   October–March 9.30 a.m.–5 p.m.

CHURCHES

OLD ST PAUL'S EPISCOPAL CHURCH
Address: 39 Jeffrey Street, Edinburgh EH1 1DH
Telephone: 0131 556 3332
Email: office@osp.org.uk
Website: www.osp.org.uk
Open: Monday–Saturday 8 a.m.–6 p.m.

MANSFIELD TRAQUAIR CENTRE
Address: 15 Mansfield Place, Edinburgh EH3 6BB
Telephone: 0131 555 8475
Email: enquries@heritageportfolio.co.uk
Website: www.mansfieldtraquair.co.uk
Open: second Sunday of each month 1–4 p.m.

FREE ST COLUMBA'S CHURCH
Address: 1 Johnston Terrace, Edinburgh, EH1 2PW
Telephone: 0131 225 3505
Email: derek@stcolumbas.info
Website: www.stcolumbas.info
Open: By appointment.

ST JOHN'S CHURCH
Address: Princes Street, Edinburgh EH2 4BJ
Telephone: 0131 229 7565
Email: office@stjohns-edinburgh.org.uk
Website: www.stjohns-edinburgh.org.uk
Open: Monday–Friday 8 a.m.–4.45 p.m., Saturday
   8 a.m.–12.30 p.m., Sunday 8 a.m.–7.30 p.m.
   (seasonal variations).

METHODIST CENTRAL HALL
Address: 2 West Tollcross,
   Edinburgh EH3 9BP
Telephone: 0131 221 9029
Email: edincentralhall@btinternet.com
Website: edinburghmethodist.com
Open: Regular Sunday morning services or by
   appointment.

THISTLE CHAPEL, ST GILES' CATHEDRAL
Address: St Giles' Cathedral, Edinburgh, EH1 1RE
Telephone: 0131 225 9442
Email: info@stgilescathedral.org.uk
Website: www.stgilescathedral.org.uk/history/
   thistlechapel.html
Open: Monday–Friday 9 a.m.–7 p.m., Saturday 9 a.m.–
   5 p.m., Sunday 1–5 p.m. and for services
   (October–April closes at 5 p.m. on weekdays.).

BARCLAY VIEWFORTH CHURCH
Address: 1 Wright's Houses, Bruntsfield, Edinburgh
   EH10 4HR
Telephone: 0131 229 6810
Email: admin@barclayviewforth.org.uk
Website: www.barclayviewforth.org.uk
Open: Sunday services or by appointment.

GLASITE MEETING HOUSE
Address: 33 Barony Street, Edinburgh EH3 6NX
Telephone: 0131 557 0019
Website: www.ahss.org.uk/about/9/glasite-meeting-
   house
Open: By appointment.

SONG SCHOOL,
ST MARY'S EPISCOPAL CATHEDRAL
Address: Palmerston Place, Edinburgh EH12 5AW
Telephone: 0131 225 6293
Email: office@cathedral.net
Website: www.cathedral.net/content/view/32/98
Open: Daily morning tours during August (except
   Sunday) at 11 a.m. and
   12 noon. Visits at other times can be arranged
   through the cathedral office.

ASSEMBLY HALL, CHURCH OF SCOTLAND
Address: 1 Mound Place, Edinburgh EH1 2LU
Telephone: 0131 651 2189
Website: www.churchofscotland.org.uk/news/
   newseventsassemblyhall.htm
Open: During the General Assembly each May or by
   appointment.

PRESBYTERY HALL,
FREE CHURCH OF SCOTLAND COLLEGE
Address: The Mound, Edinburgh EH1 2LS
Telephone: 0131 226 5286
Email: contact@freescotcoll.ac.uk
Website: www.freescotcoll.ac.uk
Open: By appointment.

ST TRIDUANA'S CHAPEL
Address: 27 Restalrig Road South, Edinburgh EH6 8BB
Telephone: 0131 554 7400
Email: stm.parish@virgin.net
Website: www.stmargarets-restalrig.com
Open: By appointment, Monday–Friday 9 a.m.–5 p.m.

MISCELLANEOUS

GLASSHOUSE, ROYAL BOTANIC GARDENS
Address: 20A Inverleith Row, Edinburgh EH3 5LR
Telephone: 0131 552 7171
Email: info@rgbe.org.uk
Website: www.rbge.org.uk/the-gardens/edinburgh/
   the-glasshouses
Admission: Daily; March–October 10 a.m.–5 p.m.,
   November–February 10.a.m.–3.30 p.m.

MANSION HOUSE, EDINBURGH ZOO
Address: 134 Corstorphine Road, Edinburgh EH12 6TS
Telephone: 0131 334 9171
Email: info@rzss.org.uk
Website: www.edinburghzoo.org.uk/functions/
Admission: Daily; April–September 9 a.m.–6 p.m.,
   October–March 9 a.m.–5 p.m.,
   November–February 9 a.m.–4.30 p.m.

DOVECOT STUDIOS
(FORMERLY INFIRMARY STREET BATHS)
Address: 10 Infirmary Street, Edinburgh EH1 1LT
Telephone: 0131 550 3660
Email: info@dovecotstudios.com
Website: www.dovecotstudios.com
Admission: By appointment.

ST BERNARD'S WELL
Address: Water of Leith, Stockbridge, Edinburgh
Telephone: 0131 556 9536
Email: dorothy.marsh@edinburgh.gov.uk
Website: www.edinburgh.gov.uk/internet/leisure/
   local_history_and_heritage/monuments/
   other_monuments/cec_st._bernards_well
Admission: Sunday during August 12 noon–3 p.m.

CAMEO CINEMA
Address: 38 Home Street, Edinburgh EH3 9LZ
Telephone: 0871 704 2052
Email: cameo@picturehouses.co.uk
Website: www.picturehouses.co.uk/cinema/Cameo_
   Picturehouse
Admission: Regular screenings or by appointment.

SELECT BIBLIOGRAPHY

Astaire, Lesley, et al, *Living in Scotland* (London 1997)

Contini, Mary, *Dear Olivia: An Italian Journey of Love and Courage* (Edinburgh 2006)

Friedman, Joe, and Aprahamian, Peter, *Inside London: Discovering the Classic Interiors of London* (London 1988)

Gifford, John, et al, *The Buildings of Scotland: Edinburgh* (London 1991)

Gow, Ian, *The Scottish Interior* (Edinburgh 1992)

Hollis, Ed, *The Secret Lives of Buildings: From the Parthenon to the Vegas Strip in Thirteen Stories* (London 2009)

Mackay, Sheila, *Behind the Façade* (Edinburgh 1995)

McKean, Charles, *The Scottish Thirties – An Architectural Introduction* (Edinburgh 1987)

ACKNOWLEDGEMENTS

My thanks first of all must go to Steve Richmond, who agreed to embark upon this project enthusiastically, maintaining that enthusiasm even after several gruelling visits to Edinburgh, and having endured conditions that were less than ideal for serious photography. He was consummately professional throughout, the results of which can be seen in this book.

As primarily a political biographer and journalist, it would be foolish of me to affect extensive knowledge of architectural history or interior design, but that does not diminish the zeal with which I approached this project. Filling the gaps in my knowledge were several people, not least Professor Charles McKean, who commented (firmly but fairly) on my original list of ideas, and Ed Hollis of Edinburgh College of Art, whose own writing, particularly *The Secret Lives of Buildings*, influenced my introductory essay.

Thanks also to those who suggested interiors I had not otherwise thought of, including my aunt Sheila Dickson, my friend and fellow journalist John MacLeod, Harry Reid and Peter Smaill.

I should also thank all those who generously allowed and arranged access to the various interiors featured in this volume. Ashleigh (at Tiles Café Bar), Veronica Barrington, Barry (at Bennet's Bar), Francesca Baseby, Kate Bell, Chris Bergin, Bruce Blacklaw, Dr Susan Buckham, Kate Cairns, Colin Cameron, Andrew Campbell, Christine (at Café Royal), Claire Connachan, Mary Contini, Robert Cooper, Linsday Corr, Audrey Dakin, Bill Devlin, Frank Donoghue, Katie Emslie, Caroline Eriyagama, Alison Fleming, Nigel Foreman, Vicki Forrest, Stacey Fotheringhame, Michael Glen, Laura Ann Govan, Gemma Gray, Sarah Grotrian, Doreen Grove, Steve Hall, Shauna Hay, Andrew Henderson, Ian Hoey, Peter A. Hogan, William Hope, Kirsty (at the Oxford Bar), Toby Jones, Sam Knight, Laura (at Tiles Café Bar), Sheona Lawson, Ross Lockhart, Lorraine (at Thomas J. Walls), Kate Love, Graeme McAlister, Paul McAuley, Des McDonald, John and Felicitas Macfie, Joe McGirr, Kerry McGuire, Charlotte McKay, George P. MacKenzie, Joanne McKinnon, Professor Donald MacLeod, Andy McSweeney, Rosemary Mann, Dorothy Marsh, Sheonagh Martin, Bristow Muldoon, Arnold Myers, Ed Nash, Hazel Norcross, Linda Ogilvie, Pauline Patel, Patricia (at Loretto), Bob Phillips, T.R. Revella, Isla Robertson, Mark Rowley, Marianne Smith, Alison Stalker, Fraser Stephen, Elizabeth Strong, Gabriel Swartland, Rev Dr Simon Tibbs, John Torrance, Sam Torrens, Valerie (at Café Royal), David Weir, Patricia Wigston, John Williams, Andrew Wilson, Andrew Wright, Alan Young. Apologies to anyone I have missed, my record keeping isn't what it once was.

The book's designer, Mark Blackadder, deserves praise for his sympathetic design and layout. Thanks are also due, as ever, to the team at Birlinn, particularly Andrew Simmons and Liz Short for being so enthusiastic about this project, most likely because it didn't involve 100,000 words on some long-forgotten Scottish politician. Buildings, and particularly photographs of buildings, are so much more agreeable than boring statesmen.